Is Trauma a Massively Non-Optimal Concept?

Pain from Our Upside-Down Words vs Pain from Events Themselves

Loran Joly

Preface

THIS BOOK TOOK me a LIFETIME to CONCEPTUALIZE, involving TENS of THOUSANDS of hours of THINKING/Intuiting, using SuperMemo, Unplugging – including a huge span of experience in Nature, alone – not as part of a group of people or with any partner, not even a dog, and use of Mathematics, as well as massive idea-stimulating pain-situations, including living as a youth in the ghettos of Detroit; two bankruptcies, one related to cancer; and much more.

I have also logged more hours of collected thoughts on voice recorders than I could "shake a stick at"...

I present my views on Mathematics here, as per its usefulness, in this video I created:

"Mathematics is a powerful tool for thinking":

https://youtube.com/shorts/HwIfoS76p6g?si=4VoT4ruYkpSu_CDq

One could also say that it the views in this book, cost me a huge sum in opportunity costs, as to what I did not find myself doingn, in life.

I would mention, also, that one might ponder the phrase that we can ALWAYS correctly "judge" (assess) a BOOK by its COVER, as per the book's NUMBER of REVIEWS, or TESTIMONIALS inside it, or WHERE it has been PUBLISHED, or where the author LIVES, or his or her "FINANCIAL" standing, or what he OWNS, in the conventional sense, or its number of typos, or level of technicolor and perfection in organization of the content, or who is praising it or not, or whether or not it is a NYT Bestseller.

Naturally, this book topic, in general, does not have the "visceral" draw of "sex, drugs and rock and roll", as the phrase goes.

This book's "marketing" is massively constrained by factors such as my commitment to assisting my mother, Lydia, now 87, in a village fifteen miles away; her having been a war refugee; my being her only relative under the age of eighty, within several thousand miles; and her never having operated a computer or cell phone, and having a sixth-grade education, functionally; her having come to Ellis Island at the age of twelve, knowing no English, speaking German, yet from Poland, and called a "Nazi", by some of the other children... And by my having recently overcome cancer, as well as the cancerous bills and phone calls from collection agencies, during and after. Medical expenses for his mother and himself in the past few years stack at more than half a million dollars. They count the cost not in dollars, but poundage: "Today's tally is TWENTY-FIVE POUNDS of bills..." Naturally, he has some ideas on this topic....

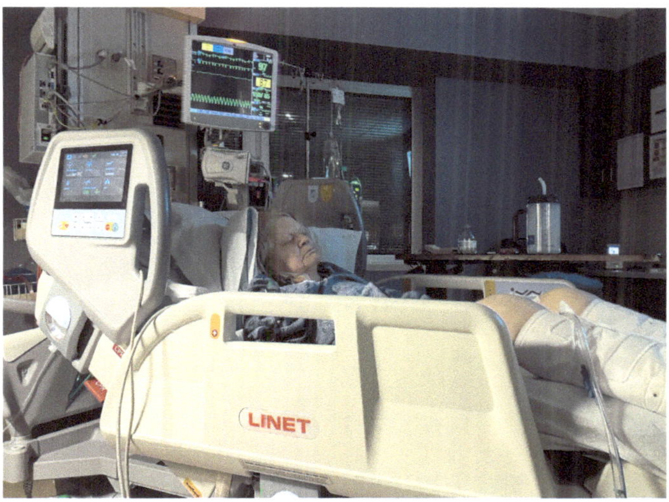

Lydia a year ago...

So, family first, book marketing second... As is a strong plus-point of many in Appalachia, in general.

Secondly, I do not believe in publishing what I call Fen-Phen books, nor in speaking "Fen-Phen ideas" (half-baked ideas, aka Ideas as per the phrase "Fools Rush in [with their Fen-Phen ideas and products and services] Where Wiser Men Fear to Tread", in general. More on that, some other time. Aka "HALF-BAKED items"... I sit and sit on material until it GELS ... until contradictions in topic matter largely subside: with the risk, that I myself "gel" first, into a final home 6 feet long and 2 feet in height, before rendering forth some seminal ideas.

***

I believe that our view of Trauma, as coming from certain venues, is UPSIDE-DOWN, and utterly non-useful. Even harmful.

Views can differ.

I think of the view of a physician somewhat outside of traditional views in some respects, Gabor Mate, MD, whom I have viewed many videos from, and what with a one hundred dollar course from him, regarding trauma:

Gabor Mate is a Jewish refugee from Europe:

"Gabor Mate - Trauma Is Not What Happens to You, It Is What Happens Inside You":

https://youtu.be/nmJOuTAk09g?si=OofcpWJB9Pc27v6Q

Then, there are the views of Prof. Sam Vaknin, a Jewish man with a Ph.D. in Physics:

Prof. Sam Vaknin:

https://www.youtube.com/@samvaknin

Also, from an Eastern perspective, the views of this Jewish analyst turned animal "analyst", having moved to New Zealand.

"Jeffrey Masson - Lessons from Gurus, Psychoanalysts and Animals":

https://youtu.be/yVw4kKoa5ac?si=wm4V00Ec-H6Mi8fA

"Animals Teach Us: Life, Love and Values, with Jeffrey Masson":

https://youtu.be/IJz8H4abONk?si=YW70ITH-sSLzUwk_

Note: Desmond Morris challenges the anthropocentric view, suggesting that our biological makeup heavily influences our societal structures rather than the other way around.

See his book "The Naked Ape".

https://www.enotes.com/topics/naked-ape#summary-summary

So, I base my ideas from many areas, including having undergone 150 sessions of psychoanalysis in my twenties, after seven years' time in the U.S. Army, including time as a tank platoon leader in Germany, and having been Airborne qualified.

The first analyst I saw was a physician in Kentucky, whom I saw for fifty sessions. The second one I saw, was in La Jolla, California, just on the edge of San Diego; a Jewish medical doctor, he and I worked six days a week for one hundred sessions.

My father also wrote his Ph.D. dissertation, in the area of English Literature, on "James Joyce: the Jewish Element".

***

I wish I could present this slim volume in the manner it may deserve:

in a Concert Hall, say, not venues somewhat less.

Yet, I have not the moneys at present, to do it justice as per such, and by the time I did, I might be long gone.

Perhaps the most I can say, of publishing and life in general, is that somewhat vague yet pregnant phrase, "It is what it is".

So, this is presented in a different wrapper than some books of equal or more acumen: one of "JUDGE a BOOK by its ORIGINS, vs "JUDGE a BOOK by its NUMBER of REVIEWS, TESTIMONIALS, sign-offs by famous personalities, or how much money one has in a bank account, or how "handsome" or "beautiful" one is said to be, or what movies one was in, and what the gross was for those movies, too.

It also is not to be evaluated by how many tickets sold to a basketball or football game, or boxing match....

Contents

Chapter One

Are We a Member of the "I am a VICTIM/I Have Been TRAUMATIZED/LIFE is UNFAIR/I DESERVE MORE" Club"?

How many people are NOT saying "I'VE been 'VICTIMIZED'"?

How many are NOT saying "LIFE is SO 'UNFAIR'"?

How many are achieving the concept behind "FORGIVENESS"?

How many are NOT saying that "LIFE DEALT them a BAD HAND"?

This latter concept is addressed in a movie format, by Robert Redford, Morgan Freeman, and Jennifer Lopez, in the powerful, challenging 2005 movie "An Unfinished Life", with esteemed director Lasse Hallstrom.

"Stoic and heartbroken, Einar Gilkyson (Redford) quietly lives in the rugged Wyoming ranchlands alongside his only trusted friend, Mitch Bradley (Freeman). Then, suddenly, the woman he blames for the death of his only son arrives at his door, broke, desperate, and with a granddaughter he's never known." (YouTube Movies and TV comments)

"I know people everywhere that THOUGHT THEY GOT DEALT a BAD HAND".

Could we say, even, "There are MANY who say that they are VICTIMS, or "have" "TRAUMA", and then STAY STUCK, FOREVER, in this FRAMEWORK?

https://youtu.be/A1NLVAWMEo8?si=yHek5btV5EONbErU

I once knew a woman who had "been in therapy" for decades, and called herself a "Therapy Junkie". Could there be such a thing as a concept like "Trauma Junkie", also?

Chapter Two

"Freud Under Analysis" - Video Link With Actual Footage of Freud

"Freud Under Analysis": https://youtu.be/gpIG6Dxd4LU?si=JBIEeXFdOWEWD_Gx

"Old film I found explaining how Freud's ideas came to the attention of the world. Some authentic footage is included, as well as the last recording of his voice. Worth watching. Some part of the beginning of the film was trimmed off accidentally."

Chapter Three

Stop Blaming Others, Says Jim Rohn

The speaker Jim Rohn, who grew up on an Idaho farm, has said:

"Stop Blaming Others | The Speech That Changed Everything - Jim Rohn Motivation":

("No body owes you any thing!"):

https://youtu.be/ZV8EqvNZ6pU?si=9MAyQaZk4RAJvX5J

"In this powerful speech, legendary motivational speaker Jim Rohn delivers his most transformative message about taking responsibility and stopping the blame game. This life-changing talk has impacted millions of lives and continues to be one of the most important messages for success and personal development."

► Stop Blaming Others | The Speech That Changed Everything - Jim Rohn Motivation

KEY LESSONS FROM JIM ROHN:

- Why blaming others keeps you stuck in life
- How to take full responsibility for your success
- The moment everything changes in your life
- Why successful people never make excuses
- The power of personal accountability
- How to break free from victim mentality
- The true secret to lasting success

"It's not what happens that determines the quality of your life, it's what you do about what happens." - Jim Rohn

Chapter Four

Trauma is a Term We Use ONLY in Conjunction With a HUMAN BEING Involved

We NEVER, EVER utilize the term "TRAUMA", or "HAVING been 'VICTIMIZED'", when it comes to any PAINS "SUFFERED" by way of "anything" associated with a NON-HUMAN "factor".

Wherein the SYMBOLS we UTILIZE to TALK of such, are strictly and completely DETERMINISTIC in scope, and thus are IN LINE with REALITY as per The Laws of the Universe.

- **DEATH DUE to "DEATH DUE to 'NATURAL'**

Causes", aka Death by TELOMERE SHORTENING.

- a TORNADO.
- a BURN from FIRE or a HOT LIQUID, in and of itself.
- a FALL onto the ground.
- The EFFECTS of a LIGHTNING-BOLT.
- A HEART ATTACK.
- CANCER
- a STROKE.
- DEMENTIA.
- Death (in a sense) due to NEVER having even been CONCEIVED, to begin with.

Chapter Five

We May VIEW a Pain as TRAUMA When We "FRAME " Our Pains as HAVING a FREE WILL COMPONENT

Yes, to frame a pain-source with FREE WILL – using SYMBOLS that have a FREE WILL COMPONENT – is to massively ADD TO the original pain-stimulus by ADDING FEAR and ANGER components...

Hence MULTIPLYING the pain by a factor of NINE or TEN, say.... My personal estimation, of course...

We might say, regarding DEATH, say, that we all would PREFER to live FOREVER.

We thus consider it UNDESIRABLE to NOT live forever.

HOWEVER, we do NOT "go about our lives", saying it is TRAUMATIC that we humans ARE, in fact, GOING to Die, someday.

Similarly, we do not PREFER to ENDURE the pains of a TORNADO or HURRICANE, but we do NOT call such pains, "TRAUMA", INDUCED by NATURE.

It being ONLY when a HUMAN BEING is somehow TIED INTO it all, that we start to utilize FREE WILL SYMBOLIC conceptualizing, and in turn, deem such,

"TRAUMATIC"; "UNFAIR"; "HORRENDOUS", "VICTIMIZING".

"It was 'FEMA's 'fault'"; "It was the WEATHERMAN'S fault"; "It was the FAULT of those who FAILED to PREPARE us for such 'calamities'"; "It was the PRESIDENT'S fault or GOD'S fault"; it was the fault of those who 'FAILED' to DESIGN ROADS that don't get CLOGGED with TRAFFIC"; "It was the fault of CELL PHONE TOWER DESIGNERS who could not provide enough PHONE COVERAGE"; it was the fault of "HAWKERS" who charged FIFTEY DOLLARS for a JUG of WATER...; it was the fault of those who failed to PROVIDE ENOUGH PORT-a-POTTIES; it was the fault of NOT ENOUGH MONEY in a "CHECK"...

"IT IS THE FAULT of those doggone FREE LUNCH providers, who DIDN'T PROVIDE me a FILLE MIGNON SANDWICH and a beer made in Switzerland, chilled to 45 degrees temperature, just like I like it."

"I'M a TRAUMA VICTIM of a POORLY DESIGNED FREE LUNCH!"

Chapter Six

Thought Experiments

I would propose that we NEVER find ourselves saying, thus, that we are "suffering" from PAINS INDUCED from "SIMPLY" a STORM, or a BULLETS or BOMBS or MINEFIELDS, or thus, "WAR", and term such, "TRAUMATIC", and in turn, "PTSD": Post-*TRAUMATIC*-Stress-Disorder.

In my view, the terms "POST", "STRESS", and "DISORDER", tend to OBFUSCATE the BASIC SOURCE of DISCOMFORT:

Yes, STORMS DO tend to cause some people "STRESS": in much more accurate stating, "PAIN" – i.e. DISCOMFORT.

This is, of course, "on the heels", timewise, of the EVENT, which then is termed "POST", a rather superfluous term, in my estimation.

Why, for instance, would anyone term the running out of gas, a PRECURSOR of NOT BEING ABLE to DRIVE DOWN

THE ROAD? NO ABILITY to TRAVEL due to NO GAS in the GAS TANK, is ALWAYS a "follower", a POST event, and need never be MENTIONED.

The word "DISORDER", also a superfluous and confusing, even demeaning term, likely:

Many aspects of life in fact being in the eye of the beholder, as to its desirability:

Some like it hot, some like it cold:

Those who like it hot, consider COLD an UNDESIRABILE, but do NOT call "cold" a "DISORDER".

Likewise, those who "prefer blondes" do NOT consider BRUNETTES to "have" a "HAIR 'DISORDER'".

We also do not consider the reality that we all die someday, to be a "DISORDER", or a "GENETICALLY-INDUCED" "DISORDER", by way, in turn, of labeling TELOMERE SHORTENING, even, as a "DISORDER".

Indeed, if there is only ONE UNIVERSE, is Reality "DISORDERED"?

Or, if there are MANY Universes, HOW MANY are REQUIRED to EXIST, before REALITY is NOT a DISORDER?

Hence, in a proper word-"framework", "PTSD" is likely an UTTER MISNOMER.

Yes, BULLETS and BOMBS DO result in PAIN; but when FREE WORDS, in particular, are ATTACHED to how we SYMBOLICALLY REPRESENT matters here, THIS is where we say things are "TRAUMATIC", or "TRAUMA-INDUCING".

Put simply, we say, inaccurately, "PEOPLE 'Cause' 'TRAUMA', but STEEL and NITROGLYCERINE do NOT."

Chapter Seven

Blameshifting the SOURCE of our PAINS onto our EXTERNAL Environment, Rather Than Our Way of ENCODING What We Experience

I believe that the concept of TRAUMA is likely a massive OVERSIMPLIFICATION of our PAINS in our lives.

It is also likely part and parcel of how we often handle – deal with – anything that is not working well, and yet, rather unfixable for most or all people – at present, that is.

If we cannot fix something painful, we may DENY we are IN pain;

We may deny the SOURCE of the pain, too:

Hence, it being LESS "PAINFUL" to SEE our PAINS as coming from OUTSIDE of ourselves, rather than INSIDE ourselves:

For we think that all we need to do, then, is ELIMINATE the "TOXIC" OUT-side "OFFENDING ELEMENT", and we would be HAPPY.

We thus BLAMESHIFT the SOURCE of 90% of our PAINS, onto OUTSIDE aspects, rather than rather UNSOLVABLE "INNER" aspects, to seek some shorter-term solace (comfort).

We might thus also call this BLAMING – in that the SOURCE of the PAINS is OVERSIMPLIFIED and SHIFTED, as part of the strategy, onto an OUTSIDE "TOXIC" part of our EXTERIOR ENVIRONMENT, which supposedly can be EASILY FIXED by ELIMINATING the TOXIC FACTOR.

However, the TRUE source of the pains is likely MUCH HARDER, by far, to ELIMINATE ("fix"), and rather than being left to DESPAIR, OVER such, we select the more COMFORTING "view":

That the pains are coming from a FAR EASIER SOURCE:

Our EXTERIOR environment, rather than our INTERIOR environment,

which CONSISTS of our COGNITIVE VIEWING of the pains:

How we ENCODE what is painful:

as per our WORDS,

And the COLLECTION of such words, being called our MINDSET.

With a SMALLER aspect of such a Mindset being our MODEL of the WORLD, in general.

Including what makes the different GROUPS of HOMO SAPIENS, "TICK", on a MACRO level.

Chapter Eight

What We Cannot ENCODE CORRECTLY, Can Cause MASSIVE PAIN

If our encoding "devices" – the SYMBOLS we UTILIZE – are "POOR" in CORRECTLY REPRESENTING of REALITY – we find ourselves feeling FEAR and ANGER, in particular.

Furthermore, this fear and anger, I would maintain, "takes on a life of its own" that in turn, DWARFS the PAINFUL SENSORY aspects, TEN to ONE.

AS such, I believe we can say that the "LION'S SHARE" of what we REFER to as PAIN – and in turn, many SOURCES we CALL PAIN-INDUCING, we blame-shift, by calling such, TRAUMAS.

Chapter Nine

Blame-shifting our Pains

WHY do we so often SHIFT the SOURCE of our PAINS (some 90% of such, I estimate), onto an EXTERNAL "cause", rather than the ENCODING of our SENSORY EXPERIENCES?

BECAUSE this is a FAR SIMPLER strategy, in the SHORT term.

We can then LIVE with the FANTASY – the DENIAL – that we can EASILY SOLVE our pains – by simply ELIMINATING some "EASILY-eliminated" FACTOR.

For instance, the "pains", of a SENSORY nature, of being IMPACTED by a ROBBERY in a DARK ALLEY in NEW YORK CITY, could be rather simply "FIXED", by merely NOT GOING INTO blind alleys in the first place.

To fix the pain by INTERNAL-environment means, however, our SYMBOLS by which we ENCODE a robbery "experience", IS in my estimation, FAR, FAR, FAR HARDER to ACHIEVE.

https://youtube.com/clip/Ugkx9F0vnXsddAXKVvMgAZ4-GmmovS_MSo2k?si=ZszyWum1iNF9pf-1

Chapter Ten

Why is it so DIFFICULT to FRAME with our WORDS - Our PAINFUL STIMULII EXPERIENCES?

WHY is it SO HARD to "FRAME" what we EXPERIENCE on a SENSORY level, in a manner that OBVIATES 90% of what we call PAIN, and in turn, "TRAUMA"?

I would maintain that this is precisely BECAUSE the SYMBOLS to UTILIZE, DO NOT EXIST, where PEOPLE-experienced "PAIN-inducing sources", are impacting us.

For we have HEARD, that MINDSET is SO VERY IMPORTANT.

Yet, what IS a GOOD or GREAT MINDSET, if not the COLLECTION of SYMBOLS which we UTILIZE to ENCODE SENSORY EXPERIENCES?

Again, if the SYMBOLS are "WRONG", and in turn, GENERATE FEAR and ANGER, I maintain that the SYMBOLS then INDUCE 9 TIMES MORE pain, than the EVENT itself.

Furthermore, if the MISREPRESENTING SYMBOLS are rather "FIXED" in our minds, the UNNECESSARILY-PAINFUL EXPERIENCES is deemed CHRONIC in terms of its SCOPE of LONGEVITY, hence the term TRAUMA, to signify something LONG-LASTING.

Finally, we cannot simply "SELECT" words that are GOOD words – symbols – because these DO NOT EXIST, ANY MORE than SELECTING a BASKETBALL to PURCHASE at a sporting goods store, to PLAY BASKETBALL, before BASKETBALLS were INVENTED.

Similarly, one cannot SELECT the BEST SPACESUIT to WEAR for a SPACEWALK, if the very ITEM of "SPACESUITS" has not yet been INVENTED.

Likewise, we could not SELECT the "best" CAR, or TRAIN to ride, or TV SET, or WASHING MACHINE, or DVD, or COMPUTER, or iPad, or iPhone, UNTIL EACH of these had been INVENTED.

Chapter Eleven

Why DON'T We HAVE the Words WE NEED?

WHY DON'T we HAVE good words to SELECT from?

At the risk of seeming OVERSIMPLIFYING, I would say I believe that the seeming NON-AVAILABILITY of SUITABLE WORDS – ones that do not INDUCE PAIN, in and of themselves, is something of a MISNOMER.

For such words DO likely EXIST – in most cultures that are communicating with words that are "ORAL" in nature, and untainted by any OUTSIDE INFLUENCES: something that is becoming EXTINCT, perhaps, and SOON.

Supplanted with the "WORDS" that are expressed in the ARTS, such as IMAGES, and MUSIC, and DANCE.

https://a.co/d/bD8W1jq

Chapter Twelve

Village Life

In small hunter-gatherer or other GROUPS, where everyone KNEW EACH OTHER WELL, and could not ISOLATE from each other, and also did not utilize the WRITTEN symbols to act as PROXIES for PERSONAL, FACE-TO-FACE, and daily, COMMUNICATING, where one's BODY LANGUAGE was ALSO a PART of such communicating, the WORD-symbols NECESSARILY HAD to stay TRUE-to-REALITY, for personal, daily relatings NOT to evolve into EMOTIONAL DISCORD, or "UN-HARMONIOUS RELATIONS", complete with CHRONIC FEAR and ANGER, and ensuing FACTIONS and NON-COORDINATED ACTIVITIES, involving food, shelter, and other survival aspects.

I would maintain that it was the URBAN way of life, with its associated "INSULATING" aspects, and communications

STRIPPED of BODY LANGUAGE, too, which is the PRIME FACTOR in a SHIFT in ACCURACY in the SYMBOLS utilized.

Words became "TAINTED", in particular, with a FREE WILL representational ASPECT, which WOULD have produced such DISCORD, in the CLOSE QUARTERS of DAILY VILLAGE LIFE, that the villagers would have EXTINGUISHED themselves.

In an URBAN environment, however, the EFFECTS of "TOXIC" or "POLLUTED" symbols, while GENERATING FEAR and ANGER, had a MITIGATING factor, as to the COLLOSALLY toxic effects on this "society":

Wherein anyone utilizing words that "induced" PAIN, could be "gotten away with", by means of ISOLATING from those IMPACTED.

Not only that, but also, those NEGATIVELY IMPACTED, could be called sub-human, too, in terms of the impacts effected:

Those impacted negatively by such toxic words, deemed sub-human and thus, the utilizers of such words could maintain a fiction of being "caring"/"loving" people – toward PEOPLE, as THEY DEFINED People to BE: THOSE Homo Sapiens they DEEM to BE such, as per having COMPLEX THINKING:

Something NOT accorded to a "mere" COW or CHICKEN or MOSQUITO.

Chapter Thirteen

Urban Life and Farming - According to Vaknin

Might we consider these words on Urban Living – CITIES – by Sam Vaknin?:

"PhD in Physics. Visiting Professor of Psychology, Southern Federal University, Rostov-on-Don, Russia (2017-22)."

SHMUEL (SAM) VAKNIN:

https://en.wikipedia.org/wiki/Sam_Vaknin

"Vaknin was born in Kiryat Yam, Isreal, the eldest of five children born to Sephardi Jewish immigrants. Vaknin's mother was from Turkey, and his father, a construction worker, was from

Morocco. He describes a difficult childhood, in which he writes that his parents "were ill-equipped to deal with normal children, let alone the gifted".

BIO:

https://www.narcissistic-abuse.com/cv.html

https://youtu.be/5IWkz8Hyx1M?si=Pt8MR34SBicitufS

"The speaker describes a diverse academic background, including degrees in medicine, physics, and philosophy, and a career shift to psychology ..."

https://vaknin-talks.com/transcripts/Adapting_to_Dystopian_New_Normal_Interview_with_Shot_Magazine/

"The discussion centers on the complexities of the human mind and the impact of modern technology and societal changes on individual behavior and relationships. The speaker argues that the rise of narcissism and a shift towards self-sufficiency have led to a decline in empathy and intimacy, with younger generations increasingly opting for isolation and consumerism over meaningful connections. The conversation highlights the need for societal restructuring to address these issues, suggesting that while the potential for change exists, the will to implement such changes is lacking. Ultimately, the speaker expresses a pessimistic view of the current state of humanity, emphasizing the detrimental effects of a technology-driven, consumer-oriented culture on mental health and social cohesion."

"It is not the first time that we are transitioning from reality to less reality.

The first time was about 10,000 years ago when we transitioned from agriculture to cities, the process of urbanization.

The city is a virtual artificial space. It's less real than the land or the farm or the village. It's constructed according to fantasy and imagination and a plan, which is entirely inside the human mind.

In other words, the city is an extension of an image in the human mind. First, the architect imagines the building and then he builds the building.

So it's an extension of the human mind.

It's not the same with a farm. In a farm, you have the land and the land is the constraining factor. There's very little you can do.

So when you are a farmer, when you are in agriculture, you are much closer to reality.

So the city was the first time that we started to escape reality. People in the city did not produce their own food. They did not do much, actually, except administration and entertainment. These were the two main functions of the city.

In a way, the metaverse is a similar transition from more reality to less reality."

Chapter Fourteen

Summary of Sam Vaknin on CITIES

A summary of Sam Vaknin's views on Cities:

"Technology has evolved from extending human capabilities to facilitating an escape from reality, particularly since the 1990s. This shift has led to a society increasingly focused on evading reality through digital means, such as the internet and the metaverse, which serve as platforms for exploring the limitless potential of the human mind. The transition from agricultural societies to urban environments marked the first significant move away from reality, with cities representing constructed spaces that prioritize imagination over tangible existence. Modern technology allows individuals to engage with the minds of others without the discomfort of direct social interaction, leading to a preference for solitude over communal experiences. This trend of isolation coincides with the rise of digital connectivity, suggesting a deeper psychological shift in how humans relate to one another and their environments."

https://vaknin-talks.com/transcripts/Adapting_to_Dystopian_New_Normal_Interview_with_Shot_Magazine/

Chapter Fifteen

Civilized in GREATER COMPLEXITY but UNCIVILIZED in our DEVOLVED WORDS - Our PEOPLE-SYMBOL LOGIC

I can only put it this way:

Being "CIVILIZED" and "MODERN" and "PROGRESSING" is associated, by SOME people, as tied to INCREASED COMPLEXITY.

Hence, a SPORTS CAR is deemed MORE "COMPLEX" than a POGO STICK.

Yet, WOULD we say so, if this CAR EMMITTED TOXIC FUMES of a HIGH LEVEL, and COST $5.00 per mile to OPERATE?

Whereas the POGO STICK emits NO smoke and costs, after purchase, ZERO, per mile, to "DRIVE"?

WHICH is now MORE COMPLEX, MORE MODERN, MORE SOPHISTICASTED?

LIKEWISE, with our WORDS – our SYMBOLOGIES for REPRESENTING REALITY – where PEOPLE are concerned – is it PROGRESS, or DEVOLVEMENT – to have WORDSETS that may be INDUCING HIGHER and HIGHER levels of FEAR, and ANGER, even if the WORDS are seemingly "MORE COMPLEX", because they are LONGER in SPELLING, or sound EXOTIC, or are "MODERN", or are COSTLY in MONEY and TIME, to ACQUIRE?

Chapter Sixteen

Is "Modern Man" Really That Advanced?

AGAIN, it seems to me, that we tend, in certain realms, to declare, to deem, that what is BEST, is what is "MOST MODERN", MOST 'SCIENTIFIC', MOST RECENT, hence most "non-caveman", MOST COSTLY, and MOST in terms of 'NUMBER of MOVING PARTS'".

This book may have some good ideas:

"Civilized to Death".

Is Advancement solely a matter of Physical Longevity, or Complexity in terms of Number of Moving Parts, or COST?

If we live a MILLION YEARS and are NOT HAPPY, is this ADVANCEMENT, or DEVOLVMENT?

Give me a DAY of HAPPINESS, rather than a TRILLION years of MISERY!

Erich Fromm wrote, "To Have or to Be".

So, I would say I desire to BE (HAPPY), not to HAVE OBJECTS or a LIFESPAN that is LONGER than MOST people's, or to HAVE GREAT "COMPLEXITY" in the conventional sense, or FORT KNOX'S GOLD BARS, ...

Chapter Seventeen

I COULD be INCORRECT About "This and That"...

My views, in this book, are in contradiction, I would say, with what I have written in one book, some years back. I may later say more on this.

Everything I say, and others say, I believe should be viewed as an "OPINION", or "SPECULATION", or a "THEORY", or HYPOTHEISS, or MODEL, or a "POSITING" or "MUSING", or "CONJECTURE".

I do not BELIEVE in "FACTS"; I believe only in APPROXIMATIONS of Reality.

Yet, at some point, we all find it OPTIMAL to MARCH FORWARD, on what we deem "BEST" data. We COMMIT, to such data, at either the OPTIMAL time, or a NON-Optimal time; too EARLY or TOO LATE.

ALL so-called "decisions" are, in my view, made in a manner of "UNCERTAINTY". Yes, "DOUBT is GOOD", and yet, COMMITING is ALSO good.

"Feel the fear and do it anyway" – AT the OPTIMAL TIME; and too, "DOUBT is only SANE, and yet, COMMITTING, at SOME point, to necessarily INCOMPLETE, poorly SYMBOLIC-represented IDEAS, or DATA, thus, is ALSO Good...

We might see books such as "Take the Risk: Learning to Identify, Choose, and Live with Acceptable Risk " (Ben Carson, M.D.), and Risking" (David Viscott, M.D.)

Furthermore, all FACTS that are declared so in a court of law, are likely ONLY so in a certain EYE of the BEHOLDER.

There ARE thus, again, NO "FACTS", only MODELS of REALITY, some MORE useful, some LESS, in a SHORT-TERM span vs LONG-TERM span, or for only a SPECIFIC person, animal, or what have you, not necessarily ALL such.

Chapter Eighteen

How Many Moving Parts ARE There to a VOCABULARY DEVOID of Any DETERMINISTIC WORDS?

Could it possibly be said, that a Mind which is DEVOID of a STOCK of VOCABULARY words – TERMS – or SYMBOLS – that are DETERMINISTIC, is a mind that is "too SIMPLE", too "WRONG", too "UN-COMPLEX", too "UN-Sophisticated", too "PRIMITIVE", too "CAVE-MAN-ish"?

Or is the metric to be, that "BEST" is the "GREATEST NUMBER of MOVING PARTS"? The MOST in terms of PARTS-Complexity, vs the MOST DETERMINISTIC TERMS on hand, that are then utilized?

COMPLEX in number of PARTS, or complex in DEGREE of SYMBOLIC ACCURACY, in other words?

Chapter Nineteen

THINKING Symbols UTILIZED in Urban Centers Thus LOST a Key FEEDBACK Loop

To put it simply,

"SLOPPY THINKING" via "SLOPPY" SYMBOLIC REPRESENTATIONS, involving terms laden with a FREE WILL COMPONENT, in particular, would tend to be "CORRECTED" in a FEEDBACK LOOP, in a small, close-knit community – a HUNTER-GATHERER community, say.

The PAINS EFFECTED, from a TOXIC WORD that was UTILIZED, could not be HIDDEN FROM, as per any RETALIATION.

Whereas, in an URBAN environment, the TOXIC EFFECT of a "TOXIC SYMBOL", CAN in fact be AVOIDED, as per any RETALIATIORY EFFORTS.

Both by way of INSULATING oneself from the AFFECTED PERSONS, "MICRO-GEOGRAPHICALLY", and secondarily, in combination by a COGNITIVE (WORD-based) RE-LABELING of the negatively-affected persons as NOT human, actually:

"Having too little "INTELLECT" to QUALIFY as "human" – on a COMPLEXITY basis.

"Too little MONEY".

"Too little in terms of the COMPLEXITY of what they OWN, and WEAR, also, and what they DO with their TIME":

For instance, watching and enjoying a SUNSET being deemed "UN-complex", and hence, SUB-HUMAN, as per how TIME is spent.

Or too, even as per SITTING STILL – "BEING", if you will, as talked of in the title of a book by Erich Fromm: "To Have or to Be":

HAVING is deemed a COMPLEX entity which could be termed a sign of a HUMAN, whereas "mere" BEING could be misrepresented as SUB-human: the seeming "plight" of a ROCK or TREE or a COW...

THUS, it deemed "UN-complex" to enjoy anything with FEW "MOVING PARTS" – and deemed a NON-HUMAN "pleasure source".

Indeed, a humorous joke could be made, that to merely SLEEP as a comforting, renewing, and happiness-inducing "activity", could be called "SIMPLISTIC" in its SCOPE, if done on a mere BED of LEAVES or a STRAW MAT or a "COT":

But if done on a MATTRESS that is COMPOSED of FABRIC FIBRES from TWENTY-FIVE different COUNTRIES, then THIS form of PLEASURE-GARNERING is deemed WORTHY of being called "pursued" BY a HUMAN BEING.

"COWS sleep on STRAW (grass): "HUMANS" are supposedly DISTINGUISHED by sleeping – garnering pleasure, if you will, on "STRAW" that is COMPLEX:

Straw "DESIGNED" by "SCIENTISTS", and from TWENTY-FIVE NATIONS, again.... In LABORATORIES....

Chapter Twenty

Who "BELIEVES" in DETERMINISM"?

I would posit that there are those who SAY they DO BELIEVE in DETERMINISM.

Yes, as a CONCEPT.

Some may ALSO say that they are "SPIRITUAL" and "LOVING", because, as Garrison Keillor put it, they are SITTING in a CHURCH, rather than in a CAR".

Yet, are these but EASILY "PURCHASED" "NAME TAGS" that do not actually "WALK the TALK"?

Perhaps we are not "SCIENTIFIC", not a DETERMINISTIC, unless we POSSESS, in our BRAINS, a SET of DETERMINISTIC WORDS – TERMS – SYMBOLS.

To simply SAY we "BELIEVE" in "DETERMINISM" may have UTTERLY NO RELAVANCE, no MEANING, no AC-

CURACY, unless we EXAMINE the STOCK of WORDS by which one CONDUCTS THINKING, on a SYMBOLIC LEVEL.

This "determinist" is not "WALKING the TALK"?

This TYPE of "determinist" – the PSUEDO-Determinist, says their bank account has ONE MILLION DOLLARS, and upon inspection, is a CLOSED ACCOUNT, or has a NEGATIVE or ZERO BALANCE?

Rather like calling oneself a top CARPENTER, only to find out the carpenter has a BEAUTIFUL TOOLBOX made of shiny TITANIUM, and when opened up, is UTTERLY EMPTY, UTTERLY DEVOID of any TOOLS, inside of it.

Yes, a SELF-AVOWED "DETERMINIST" who has NO DETERMINISTIC "TOOLS", is LIKELY an OXYMORON!

Like a COMPUTER with NO SILICON CHIPS inside of it, but simply a METAL CHASSIS containing a BAG of POTATO CHIPS, used as a fancy LUNCH-

BOX, mislabeled somehow as a "MODERN COMPUTER".

I would refer to my audiobook:

"Freud and Determinism: Perhaps Many of His Concepts Were Flawed Because His Words Were Not Deterministic?", by Loran Joly

https://www.kobo.com/us/en/audiobook/freud-and-determinism

Chapter Twenty-One

"Trauma": a RECAP - and "FORGIVENESS"...

I would propose that "trauma" does not exist, per say.

On the other hand, suffering, DOES exist.

Furthermore, I would posit that the concept we call FORE-GIVENESS, or "FORGIVING" someone, is NOT a "DECISION", "CHOICE", some other EPIPHONE or SNAP JUDGMENT, but rather, a matter entirely of the WORDS we UTILIZE, in FRAMING a "SITUATION" – in this case, a painful situation involving a HUMAN BEING.

In both cases, I see the factor of the wordset of FREE WILL as highly PROBLEMATIC to a correct VIEW of REALITY, in terms of ENCODING it into SYMBOLOGY, that is.

We could thus consider replacing terms such as TRAUMA and "FORGIVING" someone, with SEEING PAIN tied with a

PERSON involved, as tied integrally to the CORRECTNESS of the TERMS involved.

We thus ACHIEVE "RELIEF" from so-called "TRAUMA", and achieve "FORGIVENESS", to the EXTENT we achieve a WORDSET to "FRAME" certain matters, in a DETERMINISTIC manner.

The "TRAUMA-FREE" person, the person, also, who "has 'FORGIVEN'", BEING the person with a SUITABLE SET of LOGIC SYMBOLS by which to CORRECTLY ENCODE ALL aspects of matters involving a HUMAN BEING tied in:

symbols that are DETERMINISTIC.

To CROSS OVER to seeing our pains and our limitations in a DETERMINISTIC fashion – with the TERMS by which to DO so – OR, by NOT THINKING AT ALL with LOGIC symbols, but instead, with "INTUITION" or PICTURES or MUSIC or DANCE, say, which are DEVOID of FREE WILL "THINKING" – is to have EVOLVED, in a sense, to a REALM of LIVING LIFE that could be called "MORE EVOLVED", more "ENLIGHTENED".

Yes, although not endowed with COMPLEX symbology, the THINKING of the "ARTIST", in all realms of the word, or the "INTUITER", the "Feeler", the MEDITATOR, being DE-

TERMINSTIC to the EXTENT of being DEVOID of FREE WILL SYMBOLOGY-"Thinking"....

YES, it being our WORDS that have become "more 'ENLIGHTENED", not ourselves in some OTHER fashion, perhaps.

Chapter Twenty-Two

More on My View on the Usefulness of Mathematics in Pursuing Reality

Description of my video,

"Mathematics is a powerful tool for thinking":

https://youtube.com/shorts/HwIfoS76p6g?si=5Ce_5yRz1rMAw2xy

"Mathematics is a tool, or moreover, a collection of tools. We use tools to overcome our limitations, our "constraints". To Increase our Power over these limitations. Robert Greene has addressed Power, in his book, The 48 Laws of Power. Sun Tzu also addressed Power, in his book, The Art of War. Now, at a higher level, a more abstract level, we might ponder these words by Benjamin Franklin: "Man is a tool-making animal." "The 'tools' mentioned in this quote can be interpreted both literally and metaphorically. Literally, it refers to the physical tools we've invented throughout history, from the simple stone tools of our early ancestors to the advanced digital technologies of today. Metaphorically, it can refer to the non-physical tools we create, such as systems, strategies, concepts, and ideas that help us navigate through life." https://quotes.guide/benjamin-franklin/quote/man-is-a-tool-making-animal/ One might consider, however: are not the tools of ideas, of knowledge, of Mathematics, also physical in nature, given that knowledge is also physical in nature: it is physical at both the "molecular and cellular level". https://www.sciencedirect.com/science/article/pii/S0021925822003064 Another source says: "Ultimately, memories are encoded in circuits, and the synapses are just a means for etching out these circuits," said Don Arnold, a neuroscientist at the University of Southern California. "That's what changes in the brain when a memory is made, you have this new circuit that encodes the memory." https://www.live-science.com/how-the-brain-stores-memories We have likely heard, and perhaps read, Napoleon Hill's book, "Think and Grow Rich". Toward the end of this book, he interestingly states that wealth is not necessarily best measured in dollars and cents - paraphrased. What better way of thinking, than by use of the best tools possible?"

Chapter Twenty-Three

The Author

I am a product of many influences:

Violin studies in the Suzuki violin program, MacPhail Center for Music, Minneapolis:

"Nurtured by Love DVD Preview":

https://youtu.be/ZBjKw7KOwd8?si=xsXRTBJ1pj4XZBx
C

Graduate, electrical engineering, West Point:

"Welcome to West Point: Inside the US Army's prestigious military academy":

https://youtu.be/5VQUp1ddbWw?si=IaSyCV9WvA0yAV
W6

Four years of study at Berea College, studying solely Mathematics:

"This is Berea College":

https://youtu.be/tnslBwj21P0?si=PAR5QVprAsU1xKRt

Use of SuperMemo spaced repetition software program, starting at the same time I started Mathematics studies at Berea College and then continuing on for fifteen years total:

"1.0 - Introduction to SuperMemo - Fowl's Guide to SuperMemo":

https://youtu.be/i33BTuwTgAs?si=U4FNNvzFFWT8YtAW

I wrote about this time in my life here; I possibly have the world's record on the use of the software, according to the creator, Piotr Wozniak. We corresponded several times, some fifteen years ago...

"The Very Uncommon Credential: My Fifteen Years With SuperMemo Spaced Repetition Software":

https://a.co/d/c4cQfNf

The author runs, amongst other information sources:

https://landwalks.com

https://healthbirds.org

"Mathematics for Growth":

https://www.youtube.com/@MathematicsForGrowth

"Knowledge is Power.

We all want more Power.

This channel discusses the role of Mathematics in increasing our Power, essentially.

It also will attempt to discuss, matters of how we are applying our Power, when it comes to the use of Mathematics.

In other words, what are our greatest Goals, to which we apply such Power? What is our Why, one might say, to borrow a phrase from Simon Sinek.

Now, regardless of our Why", we naturally we seek to "Grow" more Power, by "Collecting" Knowledge: we are Information-Gatherers.

However, some Information is not easy to obtain, for a variety of reasons.

So, we must "Unearth" this data, this Information. We must "Mine" it.

And this "Mining" is, of course, done - done most efficiently - with what we call Tools.

The very topic of why tools are so immensely useful, is a key topic, of course.

At the end of the day, however, we ask ourselves:

Would we select a nail-clipper or a lawnmower, to cut a lawn? The lawnmower is a better tool."

Chapter Twenty-Four

Contact info

Message@goldpogo.com

This author was greatly influenced by his time studying violin with Mark Bjork at MacPhail Center for Music, in Minneapolis, who in turn had studied for four months with Mr. Suzuki in Japan, and also studied with Josef Gingold in Indiana...

Author in back row, about age twelve, Minneapolis

I'd love to hear from you...

Me as a young tyke in Detroit

www.ingramcontent.com/pod-product-compliance
Lightning Source LLC
LaVergne TN
LVHW051130210926
848482LV00001B/39